The Agile Brand Guide to
Customer Data Platforms

Evaluating, buying, and implementing a CDP for marketers

By Greg Kihlström

Published by:

Agile Brand, LLC

3100 Clarendon Boulevard #200, Arlington, VA 22201

https://www.gregkihlstrom.com

First Edition: September 2022

The publisher is not responsible for websites (or their content) that are not owned by the publisher.

Cover Design and Illustrations by Greg Kihlström

Copyright: 2023

ISBN – 979-8-8475-3558-8

To Lindsey, whose partnership and support
continually inspires me to share what I learn with
as many people as I can

Also by **Greg Kihlström**:

The Agile Web (2016)

The Agile Brand (2018)

Ever Seeking: The History and Future of Search Engines (2018)

The Agile Consumer (2019)

Digital Delight (2019)

The Center of Experience (2020)

The Agile Workforce (2021)

Meaningful Measurement of the Customer Experience (2022)

The Agile Brand Guide to Customer Journey Platforms (2022)

Forthcoming: *House of the Customer* (2023)

Listen to the podcast

For twice-weekly insights, ideas, and advice on marketing technology challenges and opportunities, listen to The Agile Brand with Greg Kihlström podcast on your favorite podcast platform.

www.theagilebrand.show

Contents

Introduction

Welcome to this first-ever *Agile Brand Guide to Customer Data Platforms* (CDPs). Based on my experience in the marketing technology space, the area of CDPs is not only fast-growing, but much change is happening. Thus, keeping up with all the changes and developments is hard.

The purpose of this guide is to help demystify what CDPs are, how they are used, and the benefits they can bring your organization. Whether you are a complete beginner to the world of Customer Data Platforms, or if you are just needing to get up to speed because of a new initiative at your organization, you should be able to find some ideas and insights in the pages that follow.

Some of the thoughts and ideas shared in the following pages are pulled directly from my book, *House of the Customer*, and others have been adapted from some of my other writings for leading publications. There are many thoughts here based on very real and recent first-hand experiences.

Why Customer Data Platforms?

I chose Customer Data Platforms as the topic of the first of many Agile Brand Guides because of the volume of interest that the companies I work with, the leaders I speak with, and the overall industry chatter about this area of marketing technology.

There are a lot of software tools that call themselves CDPs and a wide variety of what those platforms deliver. Because of this, I wanted to create a guide based on the advice I give to the companies I consult and on the experiences of the marketing leaders and practitioners I speak with regularly.

Introducing our North Star Goals

This guide and its subject matter (CDPs) are centered around helping organizations achieve several aspirational goals. I call these our "North Star Goals." These are the ideas and principles that should be guiding your marketing efforts. Just as the North

Star has guided many towards their destination, these are not immediately attainable for most, though they should be where you steer your efforts.

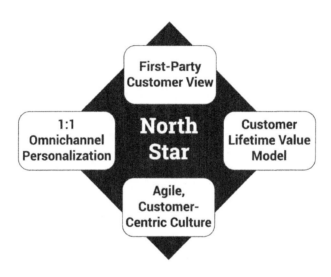

Figure 1.1.1, Our North Star

The North Star Goals can be broken down into four main goals and outcomes:

1. **One-to-One Omnichannel Personalization**

   Every customer has a tailored experience to their unique needs. Their experience is tailored from the time they become aware of a product or service until long after they purchase

2. **First-Party Customer View**

   Brands thoroughly understand their customers and governance over customers' data privacy needs.

3. **Customer Lifetime Value Model**

   Brands thoroughly understand what channels, tactics, offers, and messaging motivate customers and contribute to greater value over the customer's lifetime.

4. **Agile, Customer-Centric Culture**

   The organization continuously improves its outcomes through systematic improvements in process and delivery, driven by a culture of agility.

   If you'd like more information about the North Star Goals, I highly recommend you pick up a copy of *House of the Customer*, my latest book that discusses these in detail.

   This guide primarily focuses on the second North Star Goal: a first-party customer view, though it supports all of them.

This guide is based on research... and experience

As a consultant to Fortune 1000 companies, my work often has me evaluating Customer Data Platforms and related technologies. I have also had the privilege to talk directly with some of the leaders in the CDP community through my podcast. Additionally, I am continually researching the latest news and information in the Customer Data Platform and the larger marketing technology space.

So this book is based on my conversations, my research, and my first-hand experience of what it takes to implement a Customer Data Platform successfully.

Who this guide is for

I wrote this guide for those in the marketing and customer experience professions. While others in an organization may gain value from reading this, the primary purpose is to provide marketing leaders and practitioners with the background and knowledge needed to successfully plan, evaluate, and implement a Customer Data Platform in their organization.

For those who already have a CDP, there is value to be gained in understanding the best practices and where and how a Customer Data Platform should fit within an organization and its approach to reaching our North Star goals.

What this guide is not

While this book is aimed at marketing leaders and those tasked with planning, scoping, purchasing, and implementing a CDP from a marketing perspective, this is not a technical guide for data science or engineering teams. There are some high-level overviews which can help anyone in an organization, but there are much better resources if you are looking for a purely technical guide.

Additional resources

There are many great resources available for marketing technology professionals, including some referenced throughout the pages that follow.

You can find some related resources, as mentioned in the following chapters, available on my website, www.gregkihlstrom.com, or directly at www.agilebrandguides.com. A full list of websites and resources is available at the end of the book.

Chapter 1
First-Party Data Strategy and the need for CDPs

Customers continue to demand a more personalized experience with the brands they trust and support, going so far as to switch brands when they don't receive the level of service they expect. While consumers' expectations are increasing, the data privacy demands that eschew third-party data harvesting and identity stitching are also growing more complex. All of this adds up to a need for brands to create a first-party data strategy that allows these companies to collect information directly from consumers and provide world-class customer experiences in return.

It seems that this realization is also making its way across the business landscape. According to Nielsen's 2022 "Era of

Alignment" report, nearly 70% of marketers believe first-party data is important for their strategies and campaigns[1].

Let's look at four critical aspects of a first-party data strategy, and as we do, you'll begin to understand why a Customer Data Platform is so important.

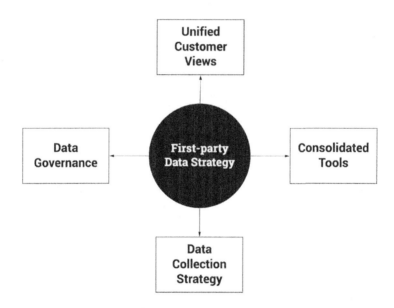

Figure 1.1, First-party data strategy components

1: Data Collection Strategy

The first component of a first-party data strategy is the approach to collecting data about our customers in the first place. If you've ever been in marketing or customer experience, you know just how hard it can be for customers to hand over even the most innocuous set of data if they don't perceive that it will be of benefit to them or if they don't trust that your brand will be a good steward of their information.

Common first-party data collection methods include:

- Traditional lead generation and customer data acquisition through email signups and other means
- Customer loyalty programs
- Brand gardens
- Subscription business models

2: Unified View of the Customer

The ability to deliver personalized customer experiences isn't possible if you don't have a complete view of your customer with the data to support that view.

The second component of a first-party data strategy is a unified view of consumers, whether they are potential, current, or lapsed customers. By having a holistic view of an individual customer, we are tying our marketing, advertising, CRM, customer service, and other data together into a single cohesive view so we can provide a better experience through personalization, automation, and tailored customer support. In almost all cases, this means the adoption of a Customer Data Platform (CDP).

A CDP can be a single, subscription-based cloud platform, or in other cases, a CDP may be a collection of purchased SaaS products and custom-built data and reporting tools. The complexity of your Customer Data Platform can be a reflection of how broad and nuanced your customer base is and how you communicate and interact with them. We'll explore CDPs in much more depth in the next couple of chapters, so stay tuned.

How important is this? This unified view of the customer is fundamental for our first-party data strategy. If we don't have this piece, our ability to deliver a winning personalized customer experience won't be possible.

3: Platform Consolidation

The same platforms and services that served your customers more generalized content or relied on third-party data services need to be rethought, sometimes from the ground up.

The third component of a first-party data strategy requires us to look at the platforms built and integrated to utilize the unified customer profile. With a Customer Data Platform (CDP) at the core, a solid first-party data strategy consolidates outdated or redundant platforms while enabling other advanced marketing tools like customer journey orchestration and next-best-action tools to provide a more personalized experience. Customer experience leaders prioritize investments in CDPs, as shown by recent research by Medallia that surveyed 583 marketing and CX professionals worldwide. They found that 55% of organizations that identified as CX leaders (as opposed to CX laggards) were investing in Customer Data Platforms in the next 12 months[2].

When creating your first-party data strategy, it is time to evaluate the relationship between your Customer Relationship Management (CRM) system, your marketing automation platforms, email providers, your Data Management Platform (DMP), and many others. Most CDPs will easily integrate with all of these, but it's not enough to just have all the data flowing in one direction.

Instead, a first-party data strategy allows you to engage in personalized marketing and customer experience in new and expanded ways. Starting with unified customer profiles, you can build towards a consolidated toolset of personalized marketing and communication platforms that can deliver the tailored, dynamic experience your customers expect.

4: Customer Data Governance

Understanding how you will utilize your customer data to provide a great experience is a key component. However, consumers are also increasingly aware of data privacy issues that can prevent them from providing information to brands they deem less trustworthy.

The fourth component of your first-party data strategy helps your organization manage the risk associated with collecting and storing your customer's data. Fragmented data poses a risk, and inaccurate or incomplete data causes customer dissatisfaction.

The role of a Consent Management Platform (CMP) can be rather large, particularly at the enterprise level, though any organization operating globally should strongly consider centralizing this role. There are many CMPs to choose from that can fit a wide range of needs.

This is not solely about software and storage, however. The processes and teams involved in data governance can impact how a brand acts as a steward of its customer's valuable information and continues to earn their trust. Remember, data privacy is not only a regulatory hurdle that needs to be complied with. Consumers are legitimately concerned about how their data will be used and accessed.

A first-party data strategy requires planning around collecting customer data, how that data is used to enhance the customer experience, and how your brand will earn consumers' trust over time. By considering these three components, you will be able to create a winning approach to the first-party marketing and customer experience era we are entering.

Chapter 2

What is a CDP?

A Customer Data Platform, or CDP, is your customer data system of record. One of the greatest values of good data is that it can provide an objective source of truth. With multiple databases, customer records, and methods of gathering data from different parts of the customer journey, how can an organization know what to rely on as that one source of accurate intelligence?

Because of the diverse amount of information that CDPs collect and how they can take both structured and unstructured data to form a unified view of a customer, you can think of a Customer Data Platform as your source of truth about an individual. CRMs can benefit from this data through integrations and pulling select pieces of information into a record. Still, the holistic view that a CDP creates puts it in a unique position in your data ecosystem. Likewise, CDPs benefit from integration with CRMs, other systems like Data Management Platforms (DMPs), and many more.

You can think of a Customer Data Platform as a way to collect and aggregate several dimensions of information and types of data about a customer. We'll discuss this in more detail as we continue our journey, but here is a brief overview of the types of data involved:

- **3rd party data**
  Third-party data is not directly collected or owned by your brand. It is data that an aggregator collects from various sources and sells as a package to augment an existing data set or stand on its own.

- **2nd party data**
  Second-party data is essentially another organization's first-party data, as they gather it directly from their audience. It may include data from activities on websites, apps and social media, in-store purchase history, survey responses, and more.

- **1st party data**

  First-party data is data about your audience that you collect directly from their behaviors and interactions. First-party data is often behavioral, as it is collected as a customer takes actions such as signing up for emails, purchasing products, clicking on ads or emails, or other behaviors you can track.

- **Zero party data**

  Next, we have zero-party data. While similar to first-party data in that it is "owned" by the brand, the distinction here is that this is information that a customer has intentionally provided rather than (in the case of first-party data) collected by a brand based on a customer's behavior.

- **Consent and privacy status**

  While this is sometimes handled by a separate Consent Management Platform (CMP), a CDP needs to be at least aware of a customer's consent, privacy, and status.

  While a CDP, CRM, CMP, and other systems can work well together, ensure that your teams fully understand what differentiates them, how each is kept up to date, and what information is best gleaned from each to provide a full picture of your customer.

History of the CDP

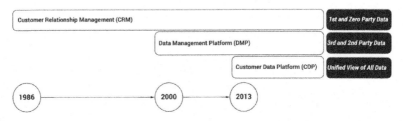

Figure 2.1, History of the Customer Data Platform (CDP)

As of the writing of this guide, Customer Data Platforms are nearly a decade old, though other platforms they are closely related to are much older. Customer Relationship Management (CRM) software first arrived on the scene in 1986[3], which enabled companies to capture customer information in a new and easy-to-use manner and utilize first-party data collected directly from the customer or by the company. A little later, in the 2000s, Data Management Platforms (DMPs) came along to collect the *rest* of the customer data[4]: third-party and second-party data that CRMs simply weren't created to handle.

It wasn't until 2013 that the term "Customer Data Platform" was first used[5]. These platforms were created to unify the first-party (CRM) data with the second and third-party data (DMPs) for a single view of customers across an increasingly diverse set of channels.

Thus, CDPs are a relatively new entry to the marketing technology landscape. However, with a continually growing set of customer channels, an increased demand to deliver personalized omnichannel experiences, and increasing privacy and customer data management needs, they are quickly becoming one of the most vital components of marketing infrastructure.

Types of CDPs

A CDP, whether a single SaaS platform or a collection of software and other services, must deliver a comprehensive set of capabilities. Gartner, for instance, separates CDP vendors into four categories[6]:

1. **Smart Hubs**, or platforms that focus on personalization and orchestration, ultimately rely on robust customer information and audience segmentation.

2. **Marketing Clouds,** or enterprise platforms that include a broad set of marketing applications, have integrated a CDP (and often an orchestration component) into their platforms.

3. **CDP Engines and Toolkits**, or platforms that focus on providing building blocks for IT and engineering teams to create their own Customer Data Platforms in either a "build" (versus "buy") approach or a hybrid approach with a composable architecture.

4. **Marketing Data Integration**, or platforms that primarily focus on data and data operations connectivity and ease of integration across multiple channels.

While most naming conventions speak for themselves, for our purposes, I don't think this categorization is as helpful when talking about CDPs in the abstract. For Gartner's purposes in describing and categorizing specific vendors (for instance, Adobe, Oracle, and Salesforce fall into the "Marketing Cloud" category), I think it is perfectly suited for the task.

What a Customer Data Platform Delivers

So while there are several ways of looking at this, I will provide four categories of requirements that define our requirements for what a full-featured Customer Data Platform should deliver (Figure 2.2 below). Let's review them below.

Figure 2.2, What a CDP Should Deliver

Acquiring Customers

The first category of requirements of a CDP includes things like enabling advertisement targeting or reaching anonymous customers by matching first-party cookies with email addresses where content is read, forms are submitted, or products and services are purchased. It also includes adding new audiences from second-party data sources to existing first-party data.

All of this adds up to acquiring new customers and better understanding previously unknown users across multiple touch points.

Engaging Customers

Next, we have the category of requirements related to customer and business growth. This includes the definition and refinement of customer segments based on a multitude of criteria: spending level, types of products purchased, estimated lifetime value, browsing and searching behavior, and many other types of data.

Using this information, we can then personalize content across any channel desired and drive customers towards the next best action that fits their needs and that of the brand.

28

Retaining Customers

Next, let's talk about customer retention. As we all know, it's much less expensive to keep existing customers than to acquire new ones. In fact, second only to "higher revenue" (58% of respondents), the second highest expectation of a CDP from respondents from Forrester's April 2022 report said improved customer satisfaction (57%) was the expected business result from having a modern, effective CDP solution.

A Customer Data Platform allows us to retarget customers across channels, provide better customer service through data and content sharing, and perform many other functions related to a strong customer retention strategy.

Optimizing Customer Relationships

Finally, a Customer Data Platform should optimize your marketing and sales efforts, as well as your customer relationships and the experience you provide. This consists of tying marketing, sales, and customer analytics together to provide offers, incentives, and the next best actions by using a comprehensive set of data. This also supports ongoing optimization and continuous improvement over time.

Now that we've reviewed what a CDP should do for us, let's explore the components of a Customer Data Platform. Remember, this may be a single SaaS service that you subscribe to, or it may be several components you integrate.

What about CRMs?

You might be reading this and wondering what exactly the difference between a Customer Relationship Manager (CRM) and a Customer Data Platform is. Both store customer data, right?

While a CRM is also (in addition to a CDP) a platform that stores customer data, its usage is primarily by the sales, support, and front-line teams. Marketers have relied on CRM data for years as their source of customer information, but there have been several key things missing from the view that a CRM has. These are, most notably, the second and third-party data available and information about the customers' digital activity across the Web.

In contrast, a CDP is a platform or collection of software that pulls data from multiple sources (structured and unstructured, behavioral and transactional, and others) to create a single, unified customer profile. This profile is then made available to internal systems for marketing and other purposes. One of the benefits of a CDP is that it sits outside many internal systems and can collect customer and contact behaviors outside of internal channels.

Keep in mind that not every CDP or CRM falls rigidly into the above definitions, with some offering some features and characteristics of the other. While the CRM category is not new at all, the CDP category still seems to be evolving into a core definition of features. In the meantime, let's look at how an organization can use these tools together to offer a more optimal customer experience.

Different Teams Work with CDPs and CRMs Differently

Success working with CDPs and CRMs relies on internal teams understanding the strengths and weaknesses of each concerning their desired goals, as well as implementing and enforcing best practices in how information gets updated within each type of platform.

For instance, marketers can have great success with CDPs when running real-time marketing campaigns that benefit from personalization and next-best-action approaches. Because a CDP is capturing a mix of behavioral, transactional, and other data, it is able to build an accurate view of that customer that can be used to target them with extremely relevant offers and information.

By the same token, sales professionals interested in building relationships with individuals will find a CRM more helpful than a CDP because of its ability to capture the information most beneficial when building one-on-one relationships. Relevant insights can be pulled out of a CDP and inserted into a CRM contact record, but many of the things that CDP stores are details that it is difficult to act on, and the volume of data collected is easier for artificial intelligence and machine learning to make sense out of, rather than a person.

While CDPs are incredibly helpful in building customer data profiles, don't forget that your internal sales teams are using your CRM for critical business, and this information can be incredibly timely and valuable. Understanding this dynamic between CDPs and CRMs can help you understand how to deploy each tool most effectively.

Understanding the CDP Market Segment

It is also important to understand that the Customer Data Platform space is both quickly growing and somewhat immature compared to other, more established spaces such as CRM. Because of this, the expectations of these platforms sometimes outpace reality.

For instance, in the same Forrester report where 57% of respondents identified that building target segments is a primary function of their CDP, only 29% stated that they were "mostly satisfied" with the customer segmentation capabilities of their CDP[7]. There is definitely room for growth here!

This is not a reason to abandon investments in CDPs by any means. Instead, it is a caution to be realistic about what can be achieved with an off-the-shelf Customer Data Platform and where other new or existing tools may be needed to augment tools in a rapidly maturing segment.

Chapter 3

What You Need in a CDP

To deliver on the first-party data strategy we discussed earlier, key components must be implemented. A key component is a Customer Data Platform (CDP), and it is perhaps best to think of this platform in a broader sense than a single product. While many cloud-based SaaS products are branded as a CDP, few are fully featured and mature in all the needed features (more on this later in this chapter).

That said, CDPs are a big priority for many organizations. In a recent study by Forrester on behalf of Zeta Global, 66% of the marketing, IT and CX professionals surveyed stated that CDP is an important initiative within their organization[8]. The remainder of those surveyed acknowledged that their approach to customer data is more ad hoc and not part of the organization's strategic initiative. Sadly, those organizations will see an increasing gap in their ability to catch up with their competitors, who see customer data as one of the key strategic priorities in the months and years ahead. While there are other components to a first-party data strategy, as we just discussed in the previous chapter, investments in a Customer Data Platform are becoming increasingly critical, as we'll explore in this and the next few chapters.

Before we talk about the technical components of a holistic Customer Data Platform, let's first talk about what a CDP should deliver to its customers.

Customer Data Platform Components

Now that we've explored what a Customer Data Platform should achieve, let's explore the components of a CDP.

Customer Data Platform (CDP)

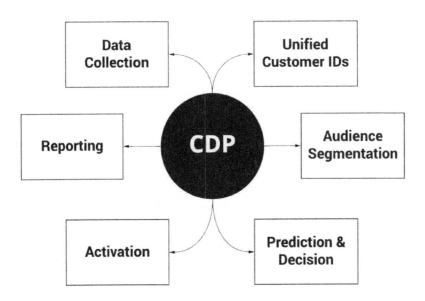

Figure 3.1, Components of a Customer Data Platform

We've discussed the critical role that a Customer Data Platform (CDP) plays in creating personalized experiences. But how do you choose the right one and know that it will include the features you need to create your ideal marketing technology infrastructure? While the term CDP is used frequently, there are many different definitions and combinations of features that these platforms utilize (Figure 2.2.2.1).

It is also important to note that because of these varying definitions of what exactly a CDP is, buyers of Customer Data Platforms can also be left dissatisfied with a platform purchased "off-the-shelf" that promises the world but fails to deliver on one or more components. In fact, a recent Forrester report commissioned by Zeta Global in April 2022 that interviewed 313 CDP users in Marketing, IT, and CX shows that only 10% of CDP owners at that time felt their CDP met all their needs[9]. It gets worse: only 1% of the respondents believe that their Customer Data Platform will meet their future needs.

I like to define a Customer Data Platform as not necessarily a single tool or product but a set of features and functionality that encompass five key areas:

1. Unified Customer IDs
2. Audience and Customer Segmentation
3. Analysis and Recommendations
4. Analytics and Reporting
5. Customer Activation

A few Customer Data Platforms have strong capabilities across these areas, though most are more narrowly focused on a specific feature set. Therefore, products branded as "CDPs" may not offer all of the features we discuss below.

Unified Customer IDs

The first component we'll discuss is arguably one of the most talked-about features of a CDP. In fact, in Forrester's April 2022 survey of marketing, IT and CX professionals about CDPs, identifying customers was the top choice (64% of respondents) among participants when asked what the primary function of their current CDP is,[10] and the second (59%) was ingesting data from various systems, which is closely related to this concept of a unified customer ID.

With so many different marketing and data platforms used by an enterprise, one of the biggest immediate challenges that Customer Data Platforms are called on to solve is unifying all of the disparate third-party, first-party (behavioral information collected directly), and zero-party (information proactively provided by a customer) data into a unified profile with a common identification number or code. In fact, in CommerceNext's 2022 Benchmarking Report based on a survey of 114 online retailers, the process of data management, or unifying visitor data and breaking down data siloes, was ranked as the top challenge businesses face, with 65% of respondents sharing this challenge in 2022, up from 54% of respondents in 2021, indicating that this is at least currently a growing concern[11]. Interestingly, the top concern of the previous year (2021) was data *collection* (63% of respondents indicated this was a top challenge that year), while in 2022, data collection decreased to 47% of respondents indicating it was a top challenge. In other words, data collection and management essentially flip-flopped between 2021 and 2022!

With this challenge solved and unified customer data in place, your CDP becomes your system of record for customer profiles, integrating with all customer touchpoints and ingesting their data. A CDP should also be able to deduplicate known (individual customers you have a customer ID for already) and pseudonymous (individual customers with whom you haven't yet associated a name or personal information already) users. Getting this unified customer ID is a great reason to invest in a customer data platform.

Audience and Customer Segmentation

The next component of a CDP is enabled once you are able to have those unified customer IDs we just discussed. While direct, one-to-one personalization and communication is our North Star, good old-fashioned audience segmentation is still a very successful way to use your CDP customer data, particularly while you are building towards that ideal state. Your Customer Data Platform should have a way to suggest new audience segments based on new insights while working with your pre-defined ones. Some platforms vary in their flexibility in either of those two scenarios. Building target segments of customers were the third most-selected response in the Forrester report I referenced earlier, with 57% of respondents choosing this as a primary function of their current CDP.

A Customer Data Platform should be your system of record for individual customer records and audience segments that can be used consistently across the enterprise. In many organizations, segments used for email marketing may differ from those used in advertising and retargeting or other channels. While there's often overlap, the inconsistency means that you aren't offering a truly consistent experience to the customer.

Integrating with your CRM database, Email Service Provider (ESP), Data Management Platform (DMP), and others means that this audience segmentation will provide the best and most effective user experience across your multiple marketing and customer communication channels.

Customer Analysis and Recommendations

This brings us to the question of what to do with all those unified Customer IDs and standardized audience segments.

Your CDP should be able to take customer data and audience segments to provide an analysis of behavior by channel, segment, and stage in the customer journey. This analysis can then be used to provide recommendations for many things, including content personalization opportunities, displaying the next best offer or action, or automatically triggering follow-up communications.

Some CDPs place more emphasis on profile unification and segmentation than on analysis and recommendations, though most provide at least some useful information to help determine what approaches your teams should take to engage customers and personalize their experiences.

41

Analytics and Reporting

With a CDP providing analysis and recommendations, the platform needs a way to share and visualize its learnings to be most useful. Customer Data Platforms are not sold as analytics and reporting tools per se, so often, their ability to provide the following is limited:

- Performance of audience segments

- Customer journey metrics

- Personalized content/offer performance

While most CDPs don't put reporting at the forefront, their customers are seeking more features here. In the April 2022 Forrester report commissioned by Zeta Global, the top response to the question of which CDP capability is most important to meet respondents' customer data goals was to provide unified dashboarding (63% of respondents)[12].

Customer Activation

Our last category is the component in which there is probably the most variance between CDP platforms. Activation provides marketing channels with content and actions to implement the next best offer or action, or set of personalized content based on the individual or audience segment's behavior.

While some have more robust features here, others adhere more towards showing and analyzing customers and segments without being responsible for triggering actions. In the latter case, it will be necessary to integrate with tools that support things like:

- Multivariate or A/B testing

- Personalization of content

- Customer Journey Orchestration (CJO)

- Integration of next best action/next best offer (NBA/NBO), sometimes referred to as real-time interaction management (RTIM)

While your CDP may not natively support the activation component, it's necessary to integrate with the right systems to take advantage of your CDP's benefits.

There are several criteria to consider as you choose the right CDP or integrate multiple systems to create a customized Customer Data Platform for your organization. Some of the

43

components mentioned earlier may be of higher priority than others. Additionally, some may be fulfilled by other systems. Other categories may require particular integrations that a specific CDP vendor cannot reasonably allow.

Chapter 4

Considerations Before You Buy

Like anything else, there is often resistance to change from legacy platforms, infrastructure, and other elements needed to make big changes happen.

While there are a few stragglers still, an example of this is the adoption of cloud computing. In 2010, this was still a $25B market but grew 535% between then and 2020. Then, again in 2021, this increased by over 35% from the previous year[13]. All along the way, I'm sure there were skeptics, or "voices of reason," that provided reasonable-sounding arguments of why it wasn't time to change just yet, even while 80% of companies were reporting operation improvements after adopting the cloud[14], or even while 82% of small and medium businesses report reduced costs after adopting cloud technology[15].

Similarly, we've discussed a lot of platforms and approaches that require a change to build our ideal marketing technology infrastructure successfully. This change takes a clear set of business objectives, measurable goals, and leadership support to happen. There will inevitably be missteps and difficulties along the way, but the organization can still benefit if these learnings are part of the process.

Monolithic vs. Best of Breed

First, some definitions. By "monolithic," I mean systems that are broad-reaching, have many features and components, and tend to work well when you buy more and more of those components.

By contrast, the "best of breed" approach refers to the approach of purchasing only the top-rated or best-matched platform or system out of each category that an organization needs.

You might think from the subheading that I already have a particular stance on this topic, but you'd be wrong! There are so many dependencies that can go into decisions to go one way or the other. For instance, while a best-of-breed approach can get an organization some amazing features, it can often require more resources to integrate these systems compared to a system that is more "all in one."

Time to value is another key consideration, but this can go both ways. Large, monolithic systems can sometimes create a quicker time to value than integrating multiple systems. In some cases, an enterprise that turns on single systems one at a time can take a more iterative approach and thus decrease time to value.

So you can see that there is no one right answer here, but your strategy needs to consider multiple considerations.

Build vs. Buy

Some organizations with more robust engineering teams (and/or vendors) decide to build some pieces needed for personalization instead of buying them 100% off the shelf.

There are many reasons why building some (though generally not all) components makes sense, though there are also potential drawbacks, as you can see from the chart below (Figure 4.1):

Build vs. Buy Comparison

Build
Pros
• The specifications for the platform are exactly what is needed, and with the exact systems you want to integrate with
• Data ownership, usage, consent, and privacy can sometimes be more tightly managed
Cons
• Time to value can be longer than off the shelf
• It can be difficult and costly to maintain integrations w/ multiple changing APIs, etc.
• It doesn't have a common API language
Buy

Pros

- The time to value is generally shorter
- Integrations are often easier with many APIs and connectors "out of the box"
- Requires less upkeep and maintenance costs

Cons

- Less influence on the product roadmap and priorities
- It may or may not work with all of your internal systems "out of the box"
- Switching costs between monolithic platforms can be considered down the road

Figure 4.1, Build versus Buy Comparison

While building some components may make sense to give a more tailored approach, an organization needs to carefully weigh the benefits and drawbacks, sometimes on a per-component basis.

According to a recent survey by MarTech, the "buy" mentality is more prevalent than the "build," at least at the moment. Their survey, done in 2022 and compared to the previous year, shows that only 11% of respondents replaced an existing commercial platform with a homegrown one, down from 13% in 2021. On the flip side, more than 25% of the respondents indicated that they replaced a homegrown system with a commercial one, which increased by 10% from the previous year[16]. The biggest reason for the replacements was better features offered by a SaaS platform (53%), followed by the need to reduce the difficulty of integrating with other systems (16%).

A hybrid approach: composable platforms

There are other sets of tools that can sometimes fit between the larger, more monolithic platforms and a build-it-yourself approach. These are what many term "composable" platforms. These have the benefits of a solid platform behind them, integrated through APIs and often utilizing the cloud to deliver services. While they can often have robust features, they also allow brands to integrate their services into larger applications that may actually combine several tools. So, as you can see, it is not necessarily as binary as "build" or "buy" in all cases. Composable platforms offer a hybrid approach.

These platform challenges and more await. Though, with a strong strategy, team alignment, and agile, continuous improvement approach, they will come together to create a well-functioning system that is customer-centric and tied to your business outcomes.

Chapter 5

How to Buy a Customer Data Platform

Now that we've gotten a good understanding of what a Customer Data Platform is, what a CDP should include, and what roles one should play within an organization, let's talk about some considerations to take when purchasing one.

Having helped many enterprise organizations (as well as a few smaller ones) to plan, buy, and implement similar systems. I approach this process in a six-step approach that ensures the correct strategic focus at each stage of the approach.

Let's explore now.

Buying a CDP

1 | Gather Requirements

First, to understand the type of Customer Data Platform you need to buy, you need to fully understand what you need and what you already have in place that needs to be integrated. This will guide you as you determine how "big" or "small" you need your CDP's footprint to be within your organization.

Remember, of course, that you may have some current infrastructure in place that you'd like to remove or replace. This can sometimes be a cost-savings (consolidation) or a simplification to make integrating systems easier in the long run.

It is also important to note that these requirements should take several aspects into account:

1. **Business requirements**

   What does success look like for the business, and how

will a CDP contribute to the success of the business and achieving strategic goals?

2. **Customer requirements**

    What is the optimal customer experience when a CDP is implemented properly?

3. **Marketing, Customer Experience, and Customer Support team requirements**

    What do Marketing, CX, and Customer Support need to be more successful in their efforts?

4. **Technology and Infrastructure requirements**

    What will increase efficiency, reduce friction, and lead to a lower total cost of ownership (TCO)? What do the architecture and infrastructure look like when all is implemented?

5. **Data and Privacy requirements**

    How will the platform contribute to overall customer data privacy initiatives within the organization?

One caution I will give here is that it is best not to involve a CDP vendor just yet in this part of the process. They may steer you unnecessarily in one direction or another, and it is too soon at this point to make a decision on a vendor. Instead, turn to your internal team or a team of expert consultants to help you build your requirements. After all, you may be able to rule out an entire category of the platform after some careful initial research and evaluation.

While I'm recommending creating a Proof of Concept (POC) as part of initial implementation, your requirements should also consider the longer-term picture. You don't want to create an amazing POC with a platform that has major shortcomings if it were to be implemented enterprise-wide. No one can predict the future with much accuracy, but make sure your requirements go beyond the immediate term so you can anticipate and rule out CDPs that won't fit your long-term needs.

2 | Define Your Ideal Workflow

While this next step is closely related to your requirements, I think it is important to call this out separately. Make sure you and your team understand what it will be like to use your CDP within your work.

In other words, if you visually map where the Customer Data Platform "sits" within your workflow, is it connecting to the right platforms, is it providing you with information at the right time in your work, and what changes will need to be made to your current workflow?

Keep in mind that there may be cases where your architecture depends on the type of CDP you choose. For instance, depending on the breadth of features in the CDP, you may either need to integrate with additional platforms in order to gain your desired functionality, or you may not. In this case, this step may proceed in parallel to your vendor selection process to a degree.

3 | Vendor RFP & Selection / Procurement

Unless you go with the "build" option discussed earlier, you will inevitably need to research, evaluate, and procure a CDP from a potential partner/vendor. Your requirements will come in handy here, as they can help you eliminate platforms that simply don't meet your needs.

Ultimately, you want to cast as wide a net as you have the resources to perform the necessary due diligence. This means that 15 vendors are too many for just about any organization to do a thorough evaluation, but 2 are too few for any and will lead to biased conclusions. Based on some initial research, I've found an initial set of 5-8 and narrowing it down to 2-3 as a final evaluation can yield good results. Still, there are many variables and dependencies here, so make sure you do what feels right for your organization and your team's capabilities and resources.

Every organization's structure is different, as well as its procurement process. So, I won't go into much detail here regarding how procurement is performed. Suffice it to say by the time you get to that point, you and all stakeholder teams should have a good understanding of the procurement scope and timing, potential overages, and other risks.

4 | Proof of Concept (POC)

This step is less common than it should be, though admittedly, not every organization has the time or resources to do it. Implementing an initial Proof of Concept (POC) project is a great way to see first-hand if a CDP will work for your organization. While it adds time and cost to the overall initiative, it can help you avoid a larger investment in a product that is a poor fit, or it can help you avoid a poor implementation of the right product.

As you define your requirements, think about what a smaller POC's scope could be to prove the model you are trying to implement. A good POC can end up saving a considerable amount of time and money in the long run.

How big or how small should your POC be? Depending on your resources, timing, and the teams involved, this could vary considerably. Keep in mind that the Proof of Concept should be big enough to demonstrate clear potential for value while being small enough to be able to implement in a reasonable timeframe and budget.

5 | Implementing & Integrating Your Customer Data Platform

With a Proof of Concept or MVP completed, you are setting yourself and your team up for success. Doing that will give you the knowledge and understanding of the product to make better decisions as you expand your CDP's scope and reach.

If you don't have the opportunity to do a POC or MVP first, you should just know that there will be a steeper learning curve. This also means that your people, processes, and platform integration will all be occurring at this learning curve at the same time.

Make sure you dedicate enough time and resources to ensure you are taking a holistic view into account. Remember all aspects that a Customer Data Platform is supposed to deliver, and ensure you and your team are thinking these through.

Additionally, work with the CDP vendor on a plan to get your teams educated, look into any certifications that might help, and consider bringing in external consultants or contractors with deeper experience with Customer Data Platforms in general, as well as with the specific platform you've chosen.

Your implementation timeline may be a matter of months, or in a larger organization, it may exceed 12 months or more. While a lot of this depends on the size of your organization, your existing marketing technology and data infrastructure, and the teams and resources available, a good approach is implementing things in an Agile, iterative manner. A phased rollout mitigates risk in many ways.

6 | Operationalizing Your CDP

With your new Customer Data Platform in place, everything will run smoothly and all the time! Scratch that. It takes work, coordination, and a mindset of continuous improvement to keep things working well. While it might seem like the hard work is out of the way once your CDP is implemented, in a sense, it has only just begun.

Make sure you start thinking about operationalizing your Customer Data Platform early in the process and proceed in parallel with this aspect during implementation. Your technical and data integrations should be occurring while you and your team can focus on the process and how you intend to utilize the benefits of your new CDP over time.

You will, of course, have many specific requirements, limitations, and opportunities in operationalizing your Customer Data Platform. Similar to the advice given under the previous point (Implementation), best practices include an Agile, iterative approach to operationalizing and expanding the reach of your CDP.

Conclusion

I hope you've found this guide valuable so far. In our last chapter, we will look at some of the things needed to implement a Customer Data Platform successfully. To do this, I'd like to use a common framework of people, processes, and platforms. We'll briefly explore what is needed in each of these areas.

People

Let's start by talking about the people component, which can have the biggest impact on the success or falling short of your goals.

First, ensure there is leadership alignment behind the initiative. This includes having an executive sponsor (or multiple sponsors) and consistent support throughout the initiative. I can't stress enough how important this is to the success of implementing a Customer Data Platform.

Make sure that the team behind your CDP initiative is diverse in skills and experience levels. While a marketing team might be the system's primary user, it will take many others to ensure it is optimized and working correctly.

Finally, ensure those people are aligned on goals and what success looks like, and bring everyone up to speed as early in the process as possible.

Process

While often overshadowed by the people or the platform components, the process is a key component of the success of any initiative, particularly one as far-reaching and consequential as the implementation of a Customer Data Platform.

Every organization has its unique blend of processes and ways of doing business. Some of this is related to the company culture, and some is a concerted effort to implement certain principles or methodologies. Agile principles and approaches, such as Scrum, Kanban, and SAFe, are highly recommended when implementing a CDP or other large-scale organizational change initiative. The iterative approach and the principles of teamwork, collaboration, and continuous improvement are incredibly beneficial and can help overcome some of the most common challenges that any digital transformation can face.

Regardless of the process you use, consistency is important, and so is a willingness to continually re-evaluate and improve what you do and *how* you do it. This is where Agile approaches work so well, though there are several ways to accomplish this.

Platform

Now let's talk about the platform component of your work ahead.

Of course, the CDP you choose to implement is a big part of this component of success. However, I encourage you to think more broadly about a Customer Data Platform because it may include a CDP that you license and integrate. But more broadly, it is a larger, further-reaching infrastructure that enables you to listen to, understand, and serve your customers with what they need, where, and how they want it.

Thus, "platform" takes on a broader context and can include many components, including just the following related to customer data:

- Customer Data Platform (CDP)
- Customer Relationship Manager (CRM)
- Consent Management Platform (CMP)
- Data Management Platform (DMP)

This doesn't include all the platforms needed to utilize customer data and serve personalized experiences. These include things like Content Management Systems (CMS), Personalization and Customer Journey Orchestration (CJO) tools, and many more.

It is best to think about your Customer Data Platform in this fuller context to comprehensively understand how data is collected, understood, and utilized. This will lead you to a greater return on your investment.

As you can see, implementing a Customer Data Platform takes a successful combination of people, processes, and platforms to serve your organization and your customers well. I hope you've found this guide helpful and wish you much success as you implement a Customer Data Platform for your organization!

About the Author

Greg Kihlström is a best-selling author, speaker, and entrepreneur, currently an advisor and consultant to top companies on customer experience, employee experience, and digital transformation initiatives as Principal and Chief Strategist at GK5A. He is also the host of *The Agile Brand with Greg Kihlström* podcast. He is a two-time CEO and Co-Founder (Carousel30 and Digics), growing both companies organically and through acquisitions and ultimately leading both to be acquired (one in 2017 and the other in 2021). As a strategist, digital transformation manager, and customer experience advisor, he has worked with some of the world's top brands, including Adidas, Coca-Cola, Dell, FedEx, HP, Marriott, MTV, Starbucks, Toyota, and VMware.

He is a member of the School of Marketing Faculty at the Association of National Advertisers (ANA), currently serves on the University of Richmond's Customer Experience Advisory Board, was the founding Chair of the American Advertising Federation's National Innovation Committee, and served on the

Virginia Tech Pamplin College of Business and Trust for the National Mall's Marketing Advisory Boards. Greg is certified as a Lean Six Sigma Black Belt, a Certified Agile Coach (ICP-ACC), and holds a certification in Business Agility (ICP-BAF).

Meaningful Measurement of the Customer Experience (2022), Greg's eighth and previous book, provides guidance on creating a customer-centric culture that prioritizes customer needs while aligning internal teams around a common goal. His previous book, *The Agile Workforce* (2021), explores the current and future state of the workforce and envisions a world where individuals thrive in a new world of work opportunities enabled by technology, decentralization, and a shift in the power dynamics between employers and employees. Greg's book, *The Center of Experience* (2020), talks about how customer and employee experience can be operationalized into a cohesive brand experience. *The Agile Brand* (2018) follows the evolution of branding from its beginnings to the authentic relationship with brands that modern consumers want and gives practical examples of what you can do to create a more modern, agile brand while staying true to your core values.

Greg is a regular contributing writer to Forbes (through the Forbes Agency Council), MarTech, Fast Company, and CMSWire, and has been featured in publications such as Advertising Age, SmartCEO, Website Magazine, and The Washington Post. Greg was named an ICMI 2022 Top 25 CX Thought Leader and DC Inno 2018 50 on Fire winner as a DC trendsetter in Marketing. He's participated as a keynote speaker and panelist at industry events worldwide, including MarTech, Internet Week New York, Internet Summit, EventTech, SMX Social Media, CX Forums, Mid-Atlantic Marketing Summit, ABA Bank Marketing Summit, and VMworld. He has guest lectured at several schools, including VCU Brandcenter, Georgetown University, Duke University, American University, University of Maryland, Howard University, and Virginia Tech.

Greg lives in Alexandria, Virginia, with his wife, Lindsey.

Resources and References

There are many great resources available for marketing technology professionals that can complement the ideas in this book. Below are a few that are related to The Agile Brand and Greg Kihlström's other work.

For other resources outside of those below, you can reach out to Greg Kihlström over LinkedIn and he can likely point you in the right direction!

https://www.linkedin.com/in/gregkihlstrom

Resources

This Agile Brand Guide is part of an ongoing and continually growing series of books for marketing, customer experience, and other professionals. Look for other Agile Brand Guides on several related topics coming soon. They will be available through The Agile Brand website as well as other retailers. For additional information, you can go to the following websites:

The Agile Brand website: a resource for thought leadership related to marketing technology, first-party data strategies, and digital transformation.
https://www.gregkihlstrom.com

Agile Brand Guides: You'll find more information on other guides in this series at this website.
https://www.agilebrandguides.com

The Agile Brand Academy: One of the newest additions to The Agile Brand family is our Academy, offering virtual on-demand as well as in-person training and courses on several key aspects of marketing technology, customer experience, and digital transformation.
https://www.agilebrandacademy.com

Martechipedia: a resource for terms, frameworks, platforms, and other items related to marketing technology. You can find information about the ideas and concepts in several of

Greg Kihlström's books here as well.

https://www.martechipedia.com

GK5A: a consulting practice for digital transformation, and marketing technology platform evaluation.

https://www.gk5a.com

Preview of *House of the Customer* by Greg Kihlström (Available January 2023)

> *If you want to build a ship, don't drum up people to collect wood and don't assign them tasks and work, but rather team them to long for the endless immensity of the sea.*
> —Antoine de Saint-Exupery

The town of Burkburnett seemed an unlikely place for a skyscraper, but as fortune would have it, a booming economy and several optimistic townspeople paved the way for just such a thing. Around 20,000 people flocked to the small town in Wichita County, Texas, in 1912. Word had spread of an oil field that promised high-paying jobs like those in so many boomtowns in similar areas.

The Newby-McMahon Building would be a monument to the town's new wealth, according to J. D. McMahon, who raised $200,000 (just shy of three million in today's dollars) to accommodate the influx of new businesses and professionals.[17] This building would put Burkburnett, Texas, on the map, and both the town's leaders and its growing population were in full support of it.

There was just one catch. Although the drawings of the building *looked* as though they had the dimensions of a skyscraper, there was something amiss. The legal documents McMahon submitted (and ultimately used in his dispute with outraged townspeople) stated the building would be 480 *inches* tall instead of 480 *feet* tall. In fact, McMahon was careful to never verbally state that the building would be 480 feet tall, and no one responsible for approving the documentation seemed to notice.

So, because of one word, Burkburnett, Texas, is home to a four-story skyscraper, known by many as the world's smallest.[18] This elaborate con stands in the town of Burkburnett, Texas, to this day.

There are several lessons to learn from this, but what I want to focus on is the need to start any transformative effort with the right plan. This includes a solid strategy, the right team for that job, and yes, the right *measurements* to ensure success. Starting a digital transformation initiative, especially one that may take years, millions of dollars, and countless hours of staff and contractor time to complete, requires that you set the right course from the start.

But let's back up first. You are likely reading this because you are either about to start a customer-focused transformation or are already halfway through. Why are you embarking on a change initiative in the first place? We'll explore this from several perspectives in the pages that follow, but here's a brief overview.

Consumers Demand More

Although 75% of consumer-facing brands claim to have good or excellent personalized customer experiences, a recent report by Twilio that surveyed 3,450 consumers around the world found that less than half (48%) agree.[19]

On my podcast, I interviewed Paulette Chafe, head of Customer Insights and Thought Leadership at Zendesk, one of the world's leading customer service management platforms. We discussed the "Zendesk Customer Experience Trends Report

2022," which found that 48% of customers in North America had higher customer service expectations after 2021.[20] Here's what Paulette had to say about that:

A lot of other companies are also reporting this increase in consumer and customer expectations. Part of this has to do with the fact consumers are owning more technology, and consumers are spending more time online, online shopping, online using social. So, they're comfortable in digital channels. We saw, in our research alone, that almost 25% of people spend five hours a day online doing various activities for personal reasons, and it's not just the younger generations. It's well across the board. Consumer comfort level and their savviness and . . . their expectations have just grown based on their experiences, and I think that's really what we're seeing right now. It's almost like it's a tipping point.[21]

Sounds like this is a challenge and opportunity that isn't going anywhere any time soon!

Change Is the Only Constant

We hear talk about how things are changing faster in our world, but as early as 500 BC, Heraclitus stated, "the only constant in life is change." Though this might seem to only grow truer each day, we can take comfort in the fact that this is how things have always been.

What matters here is not how quickly we react, but the methods and approaches we take to adapt and improve. Simply being reactive doesn't always generate the best results.

When talking about why we must build a transformative culture and a House of the Customer, we need to approach change as a given. We can't ever "set it and forget it"—at least not if we plan to be successful.

There is a long list of companies that tried that approach and ultimately failed to keep up with change. Kodak had a working digital camera as early as 1975 yet failed to capitalize on the trend when the timing was right.[22] Blockbuster turned down the chance to buy Netflix in 2000.[23] The list goes on.

The companies that thrive have kept pace with change, even reinventing themselves when necessary. IBM, known for decades as a hardware business, turned into a software and consulting services company in the 1990s.[24] Nintendo was founded in 1889 as a playing card company before transforming into one of the most successful video gaming companies.[25]

Competition Approaches from Every Angle

The word *disruption* is thrown around a lot and has been for a while. We've heard about Uber disrupting the taxi industry, Amazon disrupting brick-and-mortar retail, and Netflix disrupting the $10 billion video rental industry.[26]

But disruption takes many forms, both small and large. Competition can come from both longstanding rivals and upstarts that focus on a niche within a larger industry.

One of the recurring themes in this book is the need to balance business value, customer needs, and long-term agility. All of this helps businesses stay competitive, no matter what occurs.

Employees Need Purpose

We have seen the cost of employees who feel as though their jobs lack purpose. What many have called the Great Resignation has caused a shift in employment, with many leaving their jobs and rethinking what they want in their careers.

One of the major points I want readers to take away is that it's a win-win situation when we steer our organizations toward customer centricity. I believe that being customer focused can not only benefit customers but provide a greater purpose for employees.

So whose job is it to play a pivotal role in the transformation and continued optimization of the customer experience? According to the 2022 edition of the "Salesforce Marketing Intelligence Report," which surveyed over 2,500 marketers worldwide, 80% of marketers say their organization is the leader in CX initiatives.[27] This is in addition to the many CX teams being added as key stakeholders as global CX technology spend is expected to reach $641 in 2022.[28]

In fact, the size of the CX industry is estimated to grow at least 15% annually from 2021 to 2028.[29]

It is not just marketers or CX teams that play a key role in delivering great personalized experiences. Everyone in an organization has a part to play in building and sustaining the House of the Customer. The most successful organizations

understand this and make customer centricity just as much a part
of their employee experience as it is part of the customer
experience.

Conclusion

So why do we build better customer experiences? We build
because consumers demand it, the market demands it, and the
future of our brands depends on it.

Learn more and buy the book at **www.houseofthecustomer.com**

References for The Agile Brand Guide to Customer Data Platforms

1. Nielsen. "Era of Alignment." April 2022. https://www.nielsen.com/insights/2022/nielsen-annual-marketing-report-era-of-alignment/

2. Medallia Institute. "Uncovering the Secrets Behind a Successful Customer Experience Program: A study of more than 580 customer experience programs identifies what separates CX leaders from laggards." May 2022.

3. Ivanova, Nadia. "The ABCs of CRM." April 2019. qoreFX blog. https://qorefx.com/the-abcs-of-crm/

4. McNichols, Michael. "The History of CRM, CDP, CIP, and Everything in Between." January 20, 201. Oracle Blog. https://blogs.oracle.com/marketingcloud/post/the-history-of-crm-cdp-cip-and-everything-in-between

5. Makhdum, Abbas. "The History of CRM, CDP, CIP, and Everything in Between (video)." October 8, 2020. https://www.youtube.com/watch?v=IelblmJ1QyI

6. Bloom, Benjamin and Lizzy Foo Kune for Gartner. "Market Guide for Customer Data Platforms." Published April 8, 2020.

7. Forrester and Zeta Global. Forrester Opportunity Snapshot: A Custom Study Commissioned by Zeta Global. April 2022.

8. Forrester and Zeta Global. Forrester Opportunity Snapshot: A Custom Study Commissioned by Zeta Global. April 2022.

9. Forrester and Zeta Global. Forrester Opportunity Snapshot: A Custom Study Commissioned by Zeta Global. April 2022.

10. Forrester and Zeta Global. Forrester Opportunity Snapshot: A Custom Study Commissioned by Zeta Global. April 2022.

11. Commerce Next. "The Ascension to Digital Maturity: A Benchmark Report: Retailers Graduate from Setting Table Stakes to Scaling Long-Term Strategies." June 2022.

12. Forrester and Zeta Global. Forrester Opportunity Snapshot: A Custom Study Commissioned by Zeta Global. April 2022.

13. Jack Flynn. "25 Amazing Cloud Adoption Statistics [2022]," Zippia, accessed September 24, 2022. https://www.zippia.com/advice/cloud-adoption-statistics/.

14. Matthew Zane, "How Many New Businesses Started in 2021?" Zippia, accessed September 24, 2022. https://www.zippia.com/advice/how-many-new-businesses-started/.

15. Matthew Zane, "How Many New Businesses Started in 2021?" Zippia, accessed September 24, 2022. https://www.zippia.com/advice/how-many-new-businesses-started/.

16. Martech. "MarTech Replacement Survey 2022." July 2022.

References for House of

the Customer

1. "Littlest Skyscraper". Wichita Falls Times Record News. Wichita Falls, Texas: E. W. Scripps Company. December 30, 2000. p. 9. ISSN 0895-6138. Retrieved October 9, 2010.

2. Jerome Pohlen (2006). Oddball Texas: A Guide To Some Really Strange Places. Chicago, Illinois: Chicago Review Press. p. 67. ISBN 978-1-55652-583-4.

3. Twilio. State of Customer Engagement Report 2022.

4. Zendesk. CX Trends 2022: Improve Your Bottom Line by Putting Customers at the Top." Released in 2022.

5. The Agile Brand with Greg Kihlström podcast featuring Paulette Chafe of Zendesk. https://www.gregkihlstrom.com/theagilebrandpodcast/strengthening-business-customer-first April 15, 2022.

6. Prakel, David (10 December 2009). The Visual Dictionary of Photography. AVA Publishing. p. 91. ISBN 978-2-940411-04-7. Retrieved 24 July 2013.

7. Mary Ellen Cagnassola and Lauren Giella, "Fact Check: Did

Blockbuster Turn Down Chance to Buy Netflix For $50 Million," Newsweek, accessed October 17, 2022. https://www.newsweek.com/fact-check-did-blockbuster-turn-down-chance-buy-netflix-50-million-1575557?

8. Jim Zarroli, "IBM Turns 100: The Company That Reinvented Itself," NPR Business, Accessed October 17, 2022. https://www.npr.org/2011/06/16/137203529/ibm-turns-100-the-company-that-reinvented-itself

9. Tegan Jones, "The Surprisingly Long History of Nintendo," Gizmodo, accessed October 17, 2022. http://gizmodo.com/the-surprisingly-long-history-of-nintendo-1354286257

10. "Industry Profiles: Video Game Rentals," Encyclopedia.com, accessed October 17, 2022.

11. Salesforce. "Marketing Intelligence Report, Third Edition." April 2022.

12. "Spending on Customer Experience Technologies Will Reach $641 Billion in 2022, According to New IDC Spending Guide," Business Wire, accessed October 17, 2022.

https://www.businesswire.com/news/home/201908060
05070/en/Spending-on-Customer-Experience-
Technologies-Will-Reach-641-Billion-in-2022-According-
to-New-IDC-Spending-Guide.

13. "Customer Experience Management Market Size, Share &
Trends Analysis Report By Analytical Tools, By Touch
Point Type, By Deployment, By End-use, By Region, And
Segment Forecasts, 2022 – 2030," Grand View Research,
accessed October 17, 2022.
https://www.grandviewresearch.com/industry-
analysis/customer-experience-management-market.

Printed in Great Britain
by Amazon